DISCARD

DISCARD

JOSEPH MIDTHUN   SAMUEL HITI

BUILDING BLOCKS OF SCIENCE

ELECTRICITY

WORLD BOOK

a Scott Fetzer company
Chicago
www.worldbookonline.com

World Book, Inc.
233 N. Michigan Avenue
Chicago, IL 60601
U.S.A.

For information about other World Book publications, visit our website at http://www.worldbookonline.com or call 1-800-WORLDBK (967-5325).

For information about sales to schools and libraries, call 1-800-975-3250 (United States); 1-800-837-5365 (Canada).

© 2012 World Book, Inc. All rights reserved. This book may not be reproduced in whole or in part in any form without prior written permission from the publisher.

WORLD BOOK and the GLOBE DEVICE are registered trademarks or trademarks of World Book, Inc.

Library of Congress Cataloging-in-Publication Data

Electricity.
    p. cm. -- (Building blocks of science)
  Includes index.
  Summary: "A graphic nonfiction volume that introduces the properties of electrical energy. Features include several photographic pages, a glossary, additional resource list, and an index" --Provided by publisher.
  ISBN 978-0-7166-1421-0
  1. Electricity--Juvenile literature. I. World Book, Inc.
  QC527.2.E434 2012
  537--dc23
                        2011025720

Building Blocks of Science
Set ISBN: 978-0-7166-1420-3

Printed in China by Leo Paper Products LTD., Heshan, Guangdong
1st printing December 2011

Acknowledgments:
Created by Samuel Hiti and Joseph Midthun.
Art by Samuel Hiti. Written by Joseph Midthun.

Dreamstime 22, 23; Shutterstock 16, 17, 20, 21

ATTENTION, READER!
Some characters in this series throw large objects from tall buildings, play with fire, ride on bicycle handlebars, and perform other dangerous acts. However, they are CARTOON CHARACTERS. Please do not try any of these things at home because you could seriously harm yourself—or others around you!

STAFF

Executive Committee
President: Donald D. Keller
Vice President and Editor in Chief: Paul A. Kobas
Vice President, Marketing/
  Digital Products: Sean Klunder
Vice President, International: Richard Flower
Director, Human Resources: Bev Ecker

Editorial
Associate Manager, Supplementary
  Publications: Cassie Mayer
Writer and Letterer: Joseph Midthun
Editors: Mike DuRoss and Brian Johnson
Researcher: Annie Brodsky
Manager, Contracts & Compliance
  (Rights & Permissions): Loranne K. Shields

Manufacturing/Pre-Press/Graphics and Design
Director: Carma Fazio
Manufacturing Manager: Steven Hueppchen
Production/Technology Manager:
  Anne Fritzinger
Proofreader: Emilie Schrage
Manager, Graphics and Design: Tom Evans
Coordinator, Design Development and
  Production: Brenda B. Tropinski
Book Design: Samuel Hiti
Photographs Editor: Kathy Creech

TABLE OF CONTENTS

What Is Electricity?.................................4

Electricity in Nature 6

All Charged Up....................................8

Static Electricity 10

Current Electricity............................. 12

Circuits and Switches 14

Conductors and Insulators................. 16

How Do We Use Electricity? 18

Generating Electricity......................20

The Invention of Electric Power..........24

Sources of Electric Power................. 26

Reducing Electricity Use................... 28

Glossary...30

Find Out More...................................31

Index 32

There is a glossary on page 30. Terms defined in the glossary are in type **that looks like this** on their first appearance.

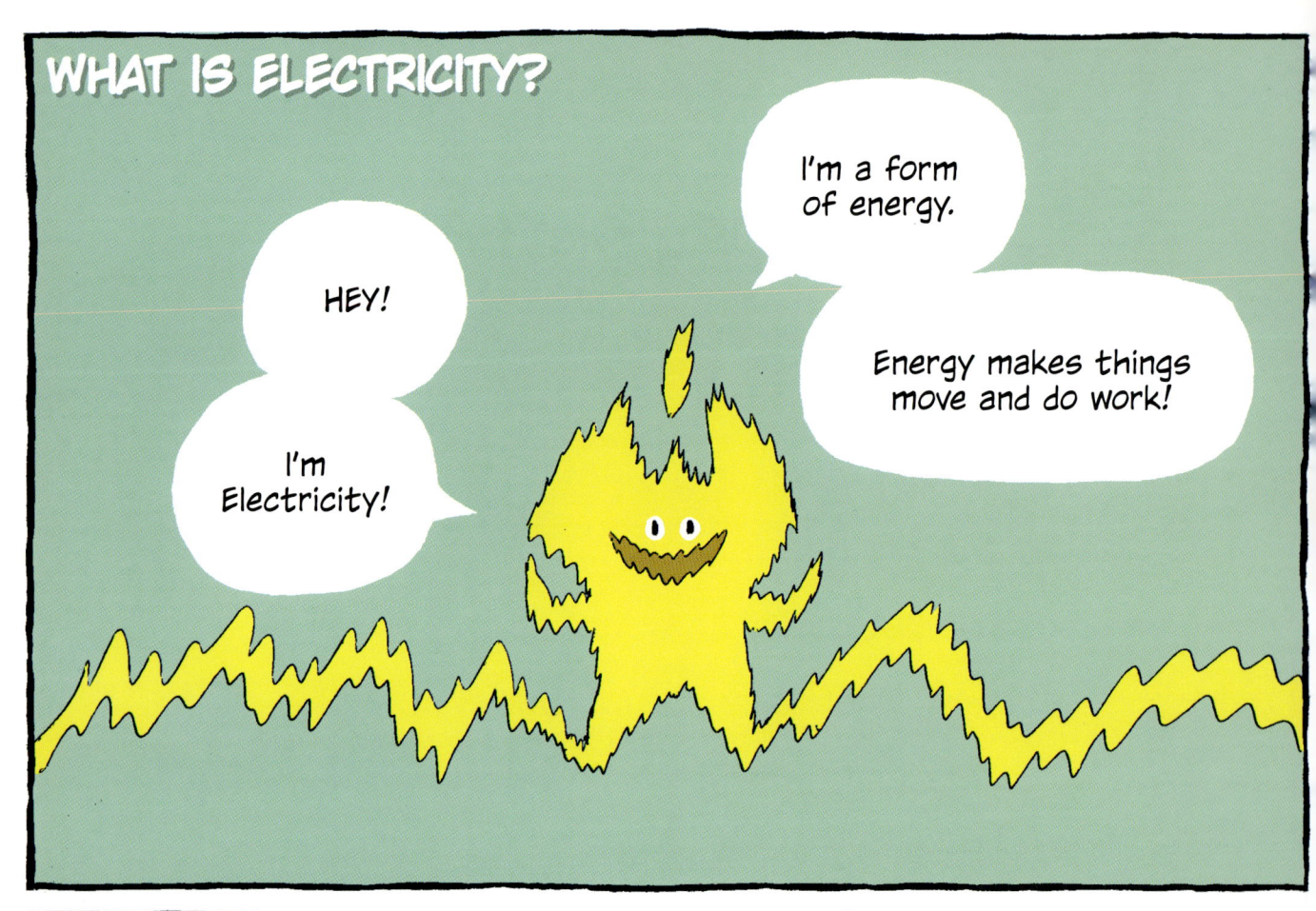

WHAT IS ELECTRICITY?

I'm a form of energy.

Energy makes things move and do work!

HEY!

I'm Electricity!

People use me to do all kinds of work...

ELECTRICITY IN NATURE

"Electricity is a part of nature."

"Sometimes, you can see me on a stormy night."

"Lightning is pure electricity!"

"Actually, electricity is a part of *all* **matter**."

CRACK BOOM

ALL CHARGED UP

All matter is made of tiny particles called **atoms**.

Atoms are made of even tinier particles.

Particles that carry a positive charge or neutral charge make up the center of an atom.

Electrons are negatively charged particles that circle around the center of an atom.

STATIC ELECTRICITY

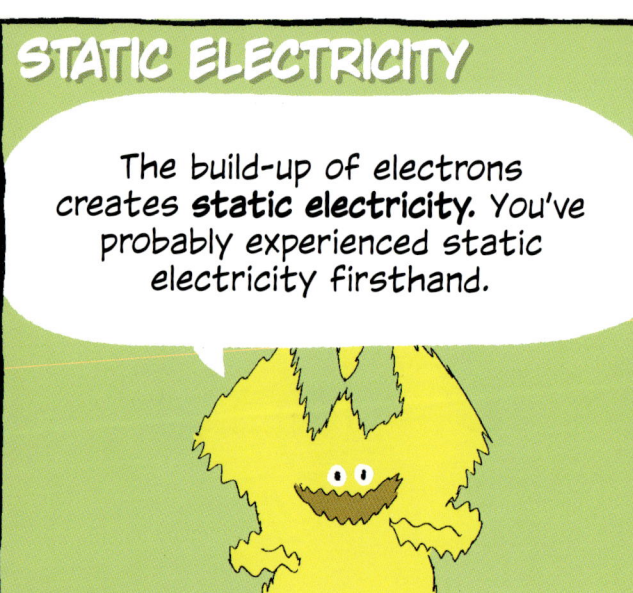

The build-up of electrons creates **static electricity**. You've probably experienced static electricity firsthand.

Have you ever shuffled your feet across a carpet and then touched a doorknob?

What happened?

You probably got an electric shock!

The rubbing between your feet and the rug causes electrons to jump from the rug to your body.

This gives your body extra electrons.

You get a negative charge!

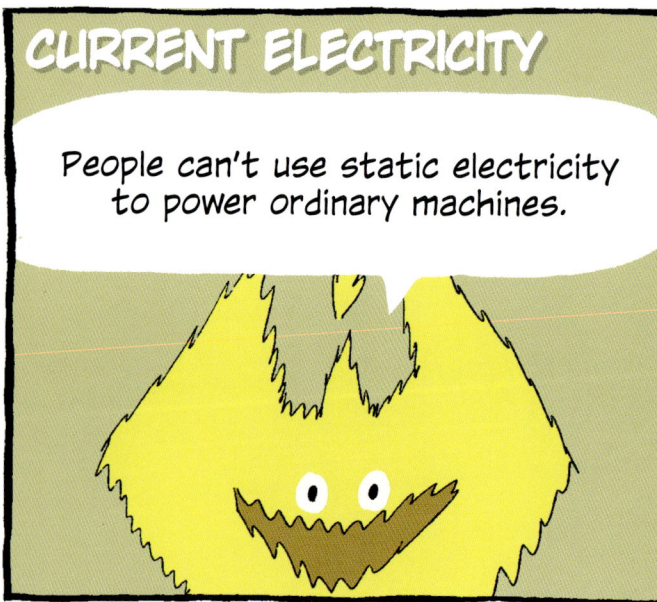

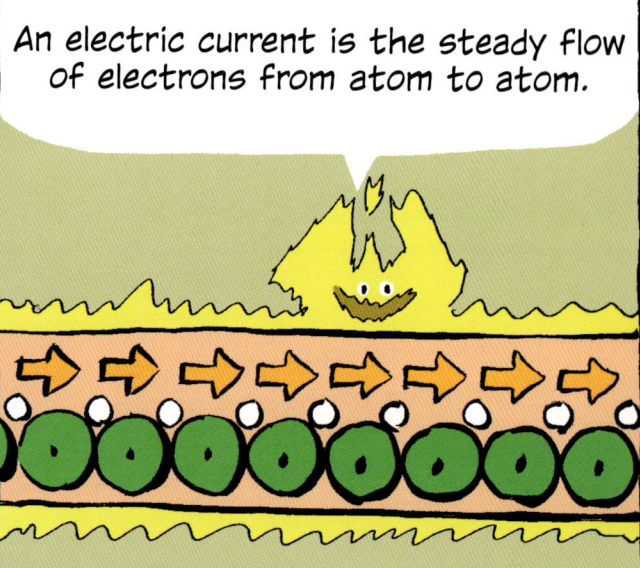

CIRCUITS AND SWITCHES

In order for this light bulb to work, the circuit must be closed.

That is, it must form a complete loop.

Otherwise, the electric current can't get through.

But what if you want to turn the light off? You can use a **switch**!

Switches allow you to control the flow of current by opening and closing the circuit.

Flip the switch to "on," and the contacts are connected!

The circuit is closed. The light is on!

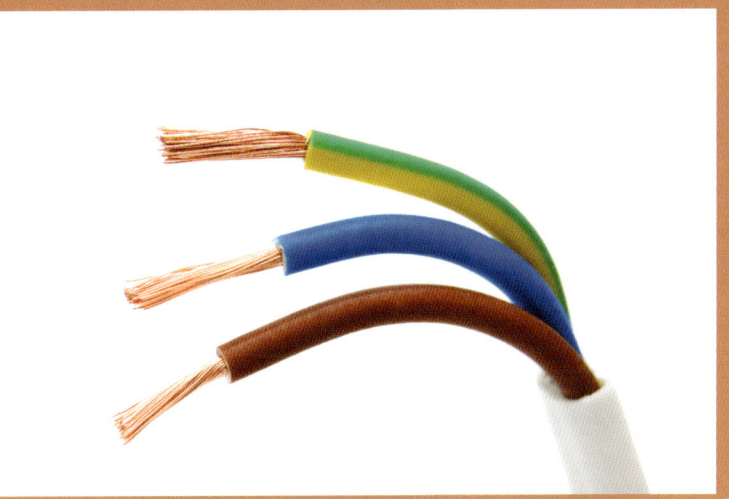

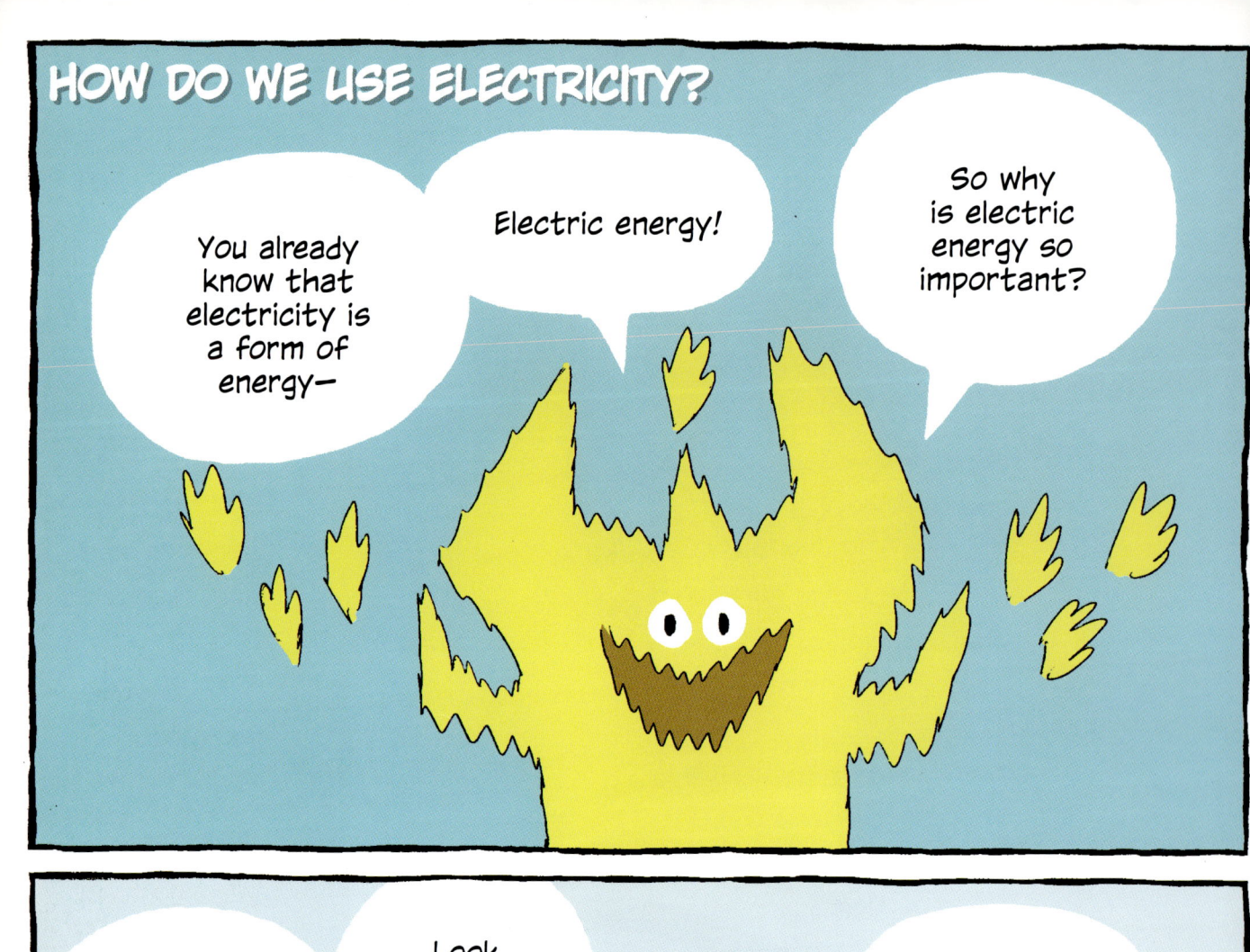

HOW DO WE USE ELECTRICITY?

You already know that electricity is a form of energy—

Electric energy!

So why is electric energy so important?

Because we can use it to make many other forms of energy.

Look at the lights around you.

They're using electric energy to make light energy!

Many people use electric energy to heat their homes or cook food.

And machines that use **electric motors** convert electric energy into mechanical energy—

The energy of **motion**! These things are possible because of me!

GENERATING ELECTRICITY

People use lots of electricity every day.

So where, you might ask, does all this electricity come from?

Power plants!

Power plants use **electric generators** to convert mechanical energy into electric energy.

These giant machines are driven by a **turbine.**

20

"These wires run through the walls of your home."

"People tap into the grid by plugging a cord into an outlet on the wall."

"Presto! The circuit is complete!"

THE INVENTION OF ELECTRIC POWER

A little over 100 years ago, people didn't have electricity in their homes.

In the 1800's, people learned to capture electricity and use it to do work.

Inventors and scientists discovered how to make large amounts of electric energy.

They found ways to use that energy to make light and heat.

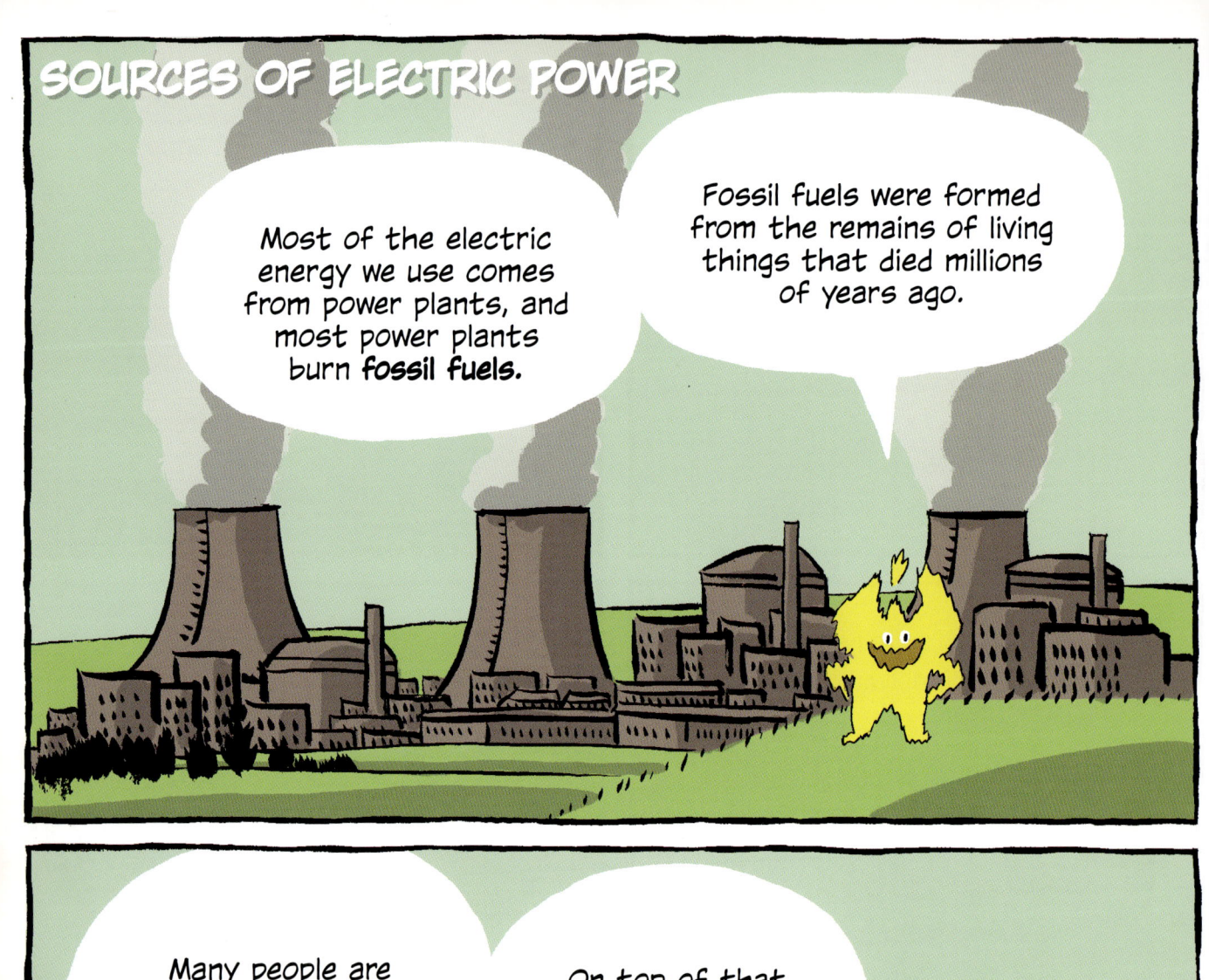

SOURCES OF ELECTRIC POWER

Most of the electric energy we use comes from power plants, and most power plants burn **fossil fuels**.

Fossil fuels were formed from the remains of living things that died millions of years ago.

Many people are worried that Earth's supply of these fuels will be used up.

On top of that, burning these fossil fuels harms our planet.

26

GLOSSARY

atom one of the basic units of matter.

circuit a path for electric current. A circuit is usually made of metal wire.

conductor something that allows heat, electricity, light, sound, or another form of energy to pass through it.

distance the amount of space between two points.

electric charge a build-up of electricity.

electric current a steady flow of electrons through a material, most commonly a metal.

electric generator a machine that produces electric power from mechanical energy (motion).

electric motor a machine that produces mechanical energy (motion) from electric power.

electron a kind of particle that circles around the nucleus (center) of an atom. Electrons have a negative electric charge.

fossil fuel a fuel formed from the long-dead remains of living things. Fossil fuels include coal, natural gas, and petroleum (oil).

insulator something that prevents the passage of electricity, heat, or sound.

matter what all things are made of.

metal any of a large group of elements that includes copper, gold, iron, lead, silver, tin, and other elements that share similar qualities.

motion a change in position.

solar of the sun.

static electricity the build-up of electrons on the surface of an object.

switch a device that opens or closes a gap in a circuit.

turbine an engine or motor in which a wheel is made to revolve by the force of water, steam, hot gases, or air. Turbines are often used to turn generators that produce electric power.

FIND OUT MORE

Books

Blackout! by Anna Claybourne (Heinemann-Raintree, 2006)

Charged Up: The Story of Electricity by Jacqui Bailey and Matthew Lilly (Picture Window Books, 2004)

Electricity by Chris Woodford (Blackbirch Press, 2004)

Electricity: Bulbs, Batteries, and Sparks by Darlene R. Stille and Sheree Boyd (Picture Window Books, 2004)

Lightning: It's Electrifying by Jennifer Dussling and Lori Osiecki (Grosset & Dunlap, 2002)

Science Experiments with Electricity by Sally Nankivell-Aston and Dorothy Jackson (Franklin Watts, 2000)

Shocking Science: Fun and Fascinating Electrical Experiments by Shar Levine and others (Sterling Publishing, 1999)

What Is Electricity? by Lisa Trumbauer (Children's Press, 2003)

Zap It! Exciting Electricity Activities by Keith Good (Lerner Publications, 1999)

Websites

Benjamin Franklin: How Shocking!
http://www.pbs.org/benfranklin/exp_shocking.html
Recreate Benjamin Franklin's experiments with electricity at this website from PBS.

Edison Invents!
http://invention.smithsonian.org/centerpieces/edison/
In the late 1800's, such inventors as Thomas Edison learned how to put electricity to work. Learn about Edison's life and work at this site from the Smithsonian.

Exploratorium: Science Snacks About Electricity
http://www.exploratorium.edu/snacks/iconelectricity.html
Create batteries and start your own electric flea circus using these online experiments.

The NASA SCI Files: Electricity Activities
http://scifiles.larc.nasa.gov/text/kids/D_Lab/acts_electric.html
Experiments and simulations will take you into the shocking world of electricity at this website from NASA.

Physics4Kids: Electricity and Magnetism
http://www.physics4kids.com/files/elec_intro.html
Take a closer look at how electricity works at this educational website.

Power Up!
http://powerup.ukpowernetworks.co.uk/under-11.aspx
This educational website from the UK Power Networks teaches kids about electricity, circuits, and safety.

Tech Topics: Electricity
http://www.thetech.org/exhibits/online/topics/10a.html
Put together the basics of electricity, circuits, and technology at this interactive site from the Tech Museum.

INDEX

atoms, 8-9

batteries, 13

circuits, 12-13
   electrical grid, 22
   switches and, 14-15
conductors, 16

electrical grids, 22-23
electric charge, 8-9
   static, 10, 12
electric current, 12-13
   conducting/insulating, 16-17
   switching on and off, 14-15
electric generators, 20-21
electricity, 4-5
   in nature, 6-7
   static, 10-11
   uses for, 18-19
   what it is, 8-9
   See also electric current;
     electric power
electric power
   generating, 20-23, 26-27
   invention of, 24-25
   reducing use of, 28-29
electric shock, 5, 10-11, 17
electronics, 5, 25
electrons, 8-9
   conductors and, 16
   in electric current, 12, 13, 21
   in static charge, 10-11
   insulators and, 17
energy, 4, 18

fossil fuels, 26

human body, 7

insulators, 16-17

lightning, 6
lights, 14-15, 18

magnets, 21
matter, 6, 8
metals, 16

negative charge. *See* electric
   charge

positive charge. *See* electric
   charge
power plants, 20-21, 26

solar panels, 27
static electricity, 10-11
switches, 14-15

turbines, 20-21, 27

water, energy from, 21, 27
wind, energy from, 27
wires, 13, 16-17, 22-23
work, 4-5

+
537 M

Midthun, Joseph.
Electricity
Tuttle JUV CIRC
12/12